# An Old-fashioned American Catastrophe: Stumbling into Love and Crashing into Life

Poems by Josh Weir

Dallas, TX

Free Tongue Press
Dallas, TX
Preferred method of contact is carrier pigeon
But if absent of pigeons, FB or Insta will do

Copyright © 2018 Josh Weir

Rights are cool, but discussion of them is hard, so we're just gonna blatantly plagiarize this paragraph from EMP press:

We find discussion of our rights – as publisher and authors – to be laughable, all things considered. Please claim this work as your own. Please republish it and sell it on street corners. Please include our material in ALL of your get-rich-quick schemes. All we ask is that you accept responsibility for any libel lawsuits. Speaking of which… This is book is a complete work of fiction. Names, characters, places, opinions, dreams, dates, impressions, monologues about a certain New York City basketball team, emotional traumas, statistics, and predictions are products of the author's imagination and/or are symptoms of mental illness. We are not in the business of accepting responsibility for anything and will deny we actually made this book and blame Carmelo Anthony at every turn.

Obviously, the above paragraph is satire. All rights reserved.

First Edition

ISBN: 978-0-578-40229-1

Design, Layout, Edits: Tom Farris
Epic Painting of Josh Weir: Steve Cruz (He runs Mighty Fine Arts in Oak Cliff. Go buy his paintings!)

if you want the truth
i am lonely
the barren moments of my now
outweigh my desire to overcome them
the bottle is easy
and makes no lasting memory to overthrow
the sick mornings are nothing
compared to the disaster of what lurks

a genius would say
 it's all too easy
to correct course
but the ship is away
and a genius is not on board

## A Real Pair

*people think i hit you* i tell her
from the stool next to her

   she nods and says *yeah probably...*

 i order us two more tequilas
and she orders two more beers
   when they arrive i slide her a shot
and she slides me a beer

  we are a good match, always on the same page

   i light a cigarette as she shakes her head
  then i say *did you know*
*Luke was going to be Starkiller*
  *before they settled on Skywalker?*

she rolls her eyes, *Josuay, you know i didn't...*

                                    i take a long drag

 and we both reach for our shots
and pour them down

  we order two more and quickly drink up

  the liquor store closes at nine

we're always on the same page

the bartender comes with the ticket
and sees her black eye
and begins looking back and forth at it and me
while i fumble
with my wallet
as i lay down a 20 and a 10
i hear her say matter-of-factly,
*he hit me*

i don't look up as we walk away
and she takes my arm

we are quite a pair

and i think she might be trying to kill me

## Sentiment

she was constantly stealing my money
 to buy clothes, shoes, or drugs
 not necessarily in that order

 it was a flaw i looked past because
she was also fucking me

 for the most part, it was a calm relationship
 unmarred by pettiness or jealousy
 we both knew why we were there

but that kind of thing never lasts long
 and finally, we found
nothing left between us
 but silence

and we fucked one last time
 with the sun pouring on us
through the open window
 until finally we came

 i closed the door quietly behind me
as i left

 and we haven't spoken since then

 makes you wonder

 where does the love go

## Faberge Eggs

the boring

  the wasteful

    the lost


this poem is for everyone

the sick man

  with guilt in the soul

                      the barefoot lonely


we need less

we need

  the coin slots

    to be fair

we can all be broken

but none of us can

be saints

## Living in This House

jobs like this are always around
out on foot, hung-over,
knocking on every door

no matter what you have they don't want it

lower the light bill?

NO!

free money?

NO!

immortality, free rent, the truth about JFK
and a handjob?

NO!
*fuck off* they say, slamming the door


a week ago, a man standing in his yard told me
to *go to hell* (he didn't know
we were both already there I suppose)
 anyhow as i walked away
i turned to see him open a tall boy
So i agreed with him he was too busy for me

we are all such simple creatures and our
lives are messy and cluttered with stupidity
and hatreds and false loves
not to mention so much intolerable boredom


and what we strive for we rarely find
every man, woman, and child enters
this world a gambler

and we are playing against a very well backed house

and sometimes the dealer drops the ball
and you come up

but the house never loses for long
and certainly takes it all in the end
when you walk out the doors
no matter who you are
   you take what you started with


nothing

## She is a Beauty

oh, that death spreading
her bleached bone beauty
all along the sidewalk

   into tiny bars
    and dark bedrooms

  her quiet whispers
   on the ears of broken people

the women twisted by ragged bitter men
  while the women that broke them flash hungry
rabid smiles from dark corners


   death, you are a whore
    and i love to love you

  with your words kicking me in the side like
  a bullet fired from grinning lips

  you always know how to perfectly break me

    telling me every day that you know the means
and moment of my demise

laughing as i run my finger
down your spine
to the small of your back

then around to grasp your hips
i like to believe its love
i've been wrong before


but i know for sure you've fucked me
and there's no two ways about it

## Now

this body tangled in time
35 billion years
in the making
from then to now the bonding of atoms
 the arrival of molecules
billions of years
to the mountain, the beast,
 the man, the woman, love, the pen,
and finally, these words
the furnace of the heavens
burning in our guts
 i tap the dust from my boots
and exhale the smoke
from well-traveled lungs
and burn that tender skin
on the top of my finger
 it hurts in a way
that makes me marvel
at the beauty of the stars

## Rejoice

i am alone with the
monster sharing silence
as we watch in envy all
that is best and bright
in this world
with remorse
and stomachs sick

we watch with crystal
eyes as the hollow
make their march with
cobbled together carts
full of all the things
they wanted
as they go to the
dark corners

people have never
learned
that love
is the only lesson
that matters

so wake up
   tie your shoes

this isn't over

there is always

a chance

## Orion

i am walking towards Orion
trying to find the remains of all these nights spent on
lust and blushing
lips stained with wine and tangled in smoke

i am walking towards Orion reaching for a lost
horizon choking on the dusty images of lost love,
lost jobs and the lost pack of cigarettes hidden
somewhere next to a liter of vodka

i am walking towards Orion
and all the beautiful storms
of lightning and thunder

i am walking towards Orion and solitude trying to
find that still small voice Elijah was so fond of

i am walking towards Orion
and waiting for supernova
the expanding light of death
and the hot boiling cloud of creation

all of this over and over again

i am walking towards Orion
and wondering if
i closed my eyes
would i finally step off the edge
and be carried out into the void
where there is no more need for prayer
or words for that matter

i am walking towards Orion trying to find peace
so that you and i can sleep if only for a blinking
moment in that far-reaching eternity
that neither of us will ever
understand

## Headed anywhere

the old courthouse is waiting to be torn down
waiting for destruction like so many of the lost souls
that have lived in its shadow
it's Friday night no... actually it's Saturday
calm and quiet in downtown midland
a more downtown looking place
than my friends in Dallas realize

i grew up here but wandering around
there are only hints of my younger days

the first coffee shop i remember
is now one block west of its beginning
and now sits directly across from the courthouse
instead of the plaza

the old plaza a place of early experimentation
skinny dipping in the fountain

finding sex on lustful lips and psychedelic
mushrooms in backpacks
The park has evolved and seems more concrete
than it ever did before
it seems so much like a hardened scar from all the
nights we cut open there

now i'm here again
  confused and out of time
  more restless than i ever was in my youth

and i know i will again move on
 maybe back to the west coast
where i can dip my toes in the pacific again
  Or perhaps to New Orleans and hurricane nights
vampire jazz lounges and tankers carrying their
viscous cargo to far horizons on drunken waves

it could be i will just end up under that tree
  where i first discovered that words
can transform anything
  the blistering sun into growth
    the pain filled nights
into sonnets and symphonies

  or the dirt beneath your toes into home

 wherever that is
  it's where i'm headed next

## The Distance

i can hear her thick accent in my head
  as she says that *i am NOTHINK* in her text
 that nobody loves me or likes me

 even though i'm the one she calls
   when everything falls apart
and the wolves
 are growling

 and we will tangle together
  and she will like me
 love me even

 for a week or so things will be perfect
  we will dance and laugh over stir-fry and diet coke

 but it won't last

 she will again kick me out

 maybe it doesn't have to last

 as i toss my bags in the car
  and dig for my pack and my lighter
 i remember the importance of seeing things through

it's cold out tonight as i curl up in my sleeping bag
the whisky almost gone

it will be gone

and i will lay here trying to remember to go the
distance

## Eating the World

hyena laughter
 strangling the sun
 as rain drops down
into the desert
 and the sand gulps
down the heavens

it is almost too much
this tangle of words
 wrapped tight around
my lacerated heart

i take her hand
 a tangible beauty

the cat watches from
his perch on the dresser
 with his slow blink

these are the moments of peace
 the world hopes for but tends to miss

## 36 years

it never crossed my mind
 that i would be around this long
and i now know that story of the weird old guy
that bought me beer when i was 18
yeah, that old guy
was probably about
the age i am now

it was back when i was young and thought
i was smart and never spent a moment
to be concerned about anything
i was indestructible after all
now i check my balls for cancer
in my morning shower
they used to just be for recreation
and looking good on someone's chin

now i'm fast approaching a time when my doctor will
want to know me more intimately
and i have a feeling it won't be like that time
with the hot goth chick with tiny hands
no, he is gruff and German with large hands and a
less sunny disposition than the goth girl for sure

i'm supposed to be aware of my age

but i still forget that i have any kind of authority

someday i suppose i'll 'round a corner
and stop caring about Star Wars plot points
more than i care about having a bank account
maybe it won't be so bad

but fuck it, i'm keeping my batman wristwatch

## This longing

this heart
tripping on empty bottle
and overflowing ashtrays

poisoned by time
  fighting to one more breath
one more chance to get it right

 i am a winner at all the things that never mattered


while the hounds growl
 and the devil bites at his tail

where is the love in these torn blankets?

 where has anything gone?

  all run away as the shadows
   sharpen their claws

If I say I'll write this down later, I'll never have the balls. Stories where the ending is so solidified seem harder to put down on paper. All the details are sitting like burning coals in my chest, and I can barely bring myself to remember them much less let them out…but they need out, someplace to go.

It's possible I should have told her weeks ago how she makes me feel but the coward in me refused to allow it.

I would drink to dress the flowers and then drop the bouquet. And I could say it's a mystery as to how one of my greatest weekends in the last four years ended with rocks in my gut, but I know what I did.

Beer and whiskey, music, exaltations of a brighter life. The ghosts of old heroes resurrected from old slumber in plumes of smoke and bellowing laughter.

She was beautiful boots and jeans electric blue shirt that made her smile seem like lightning. When the music ended we left out on country roads a corridor of trees and pinpoint of stars accented by the glow of our cigarettes. Back to the porch to sip wine listening to Ginsberg read of his America. Her head resting gently on my shoulder when Ginsberg stopped we finished our wine and fell into the hammock and into sleep with my arm around her, it was as warm and satisfying as a spring day on the banks of the Brazos. I don't think I even snored, if I did she didn't say anything.

We woke up to the glittery wave of sunlight breaking through the trees and the whisper of I-20 in the distance and made our way to coffee and breakfast while we made small talk with minor hangovers.

Saturday afternoon everything dissolving into the lake leaving me serene and almost capable of saying the right words until I see that smile bouncing through the waves towards me and I lose myself in it and the fear of not having her near me. So I clam up, shut my mouth, and only passively and playfully acknowledge her warm skin near me because I am a fool. I drink more wine and watch her tiny frame dive through the waves. I drink more wine and imagine having said something…anything, but I didn't so I drank more wine.

Late afternoon showered and dressed for another night of music and dancing I turn the corner to see her in white dress with that smile…the thought of it now brings tears to my eyes…

Country club, Texas swing, drinking double whiskey and soda laughing and listening to Gil tell wild stories of musicians   and travels. I'm oblivious now. The drink has done its work and I am telling everyone but her how I feel and how she makes me happy despite my demons. I'm so afraid she will go that I am to blind to see I am pushing her away. I'm drunk and incoherent. She is visibly disappointed in me.as I stumble back to the car I try for a moment to talk to her but it's no use, the damage is done, I fucked up.

At her house, I climb into my car and recline the seat but the heat and humiliation are too much too bear so I drive a few drunken blocks to an old rundown hotel and take a room.
Laying in a strange bed with the hurt of it swelling up in me.

Laying in strange bed I get a text from her that says she's tired of trying to look past my flaws and that this is her last and final goodbye.

Laying in a strange bed I am weeping and everything aches. The dull walls are movie screens playing in HD every way I fucked up every disgusting mistake in full and dizzying detail. The walls are tearing at me and showing me she was right to get away.

Laying in a strange bed my pack is empty and the corner store is near. I open the door and shoeless stumble out into heat and grinding gravel and broken glass. I cross the parking lot where two chatting local officers notice me noticing them.

Waking up in jail with bruised wrists…public intox charged, head pounding.

Two free calls, I use neither.

Who would I call?

Nothing to do but wait in the stark reality, contemplate the bleakness of my next move. I tell myself its good I'm locked up; it will give me time to find a way to make it up to her.

1 am, Monday morning, I am released into rainy streets, barefoot, and phone dead with no idea where I am. I find the only open station and get directions to I-20. It's a four mile walk back to my car barefoot on wet asphalt but the rain has stopped. At my car, I find the battery is dead. I sit door open contemplating ruin and wishing I could conjure nirvana and recite om and perhaps find peace in loss. There is no peace. Just this a dead battery and the eastern rising sun fighting to light the earth through weeping clouds.

And without the curled fingers of *om*, there can only be

>I am sorry.
> I am sorry.
>  I am sorry.
>   I am…

## To All the Women I Lived Through

it wasn't just you
   i'm pretty fucked up

although i'd say we might be even

  when it came to sex i never pushed
i figured it should happen naturally
  that bothered some of you
  and made you think
 i wasn't interested
   that was never the case

i've always wanted peace
something reminiscent
of zen

some of you would steal from me
  and take of advantage of my shy and simple ways

i'm certainly no saint

i'm glad we got what we could
and i'm sorry for all we lost

and if you find my love somewhere in you
send it back

this asshole needs all he can get

## Minor Repairs

*it was an accident really* i tell them

one cop looks at me and says
*man, you need an ambulance*

one his buddies laughs and says
*that, and a cup of coffee*

the older cop keeps shaking his head
and saying *sir, i need to talk to her*

*she left* i tell him *and besides, it was an accident*

and then the paramedics are buzzing around me
trying to talk me down to the ambulance

as i continued to wave them off

*i've had worse* i say

but still they clean and dress the wound

the young cop says *we need you to fill out a report*

but again i say *nothing to report*

finally they file out the door

and i watch them drive away

when they are out of sight
i call her phone to tell her
they are gone

soon she returns.

*you wield a hell of a broken coffee cup*
i say laughing

she begins to cry saying
*please don't say that
i know you think i'm crazy*

*no baby, i don't think you're crazy
you're fine*

she is fire and i am gasoline

it's a tough mixture to keep balanced

but the fires beat the hell
out of greys anatomy reruns
church on Sundays
and 9 o' clock bedtimes

The burns are worth it
and in the end
that's what matters

## Kingdom Come

*i shaved my pussy* she says

*do you wanna see?*

i tell her *of course, but let's take a shot first*

i figured it would show composure
to not be too eager
at times like that

i poured them up and we downed them

then we went to the bedroom
where she showed me her shaved glory
she giggled the whole time
*do you like it* she asked

 *hell yeah baby, that's a real flower*
and we both laughed

we began kissing and fooling around
 taking breaks to smoke and drink
or change the radio station

she danced around naked shaking her ass

 while i grinned like a fool
at that age i knew nothing of love
and even less about fuck

there was certainly some fear in those early days

but soon we were at it
 and i felt like a real champ
  i was really working things good
it was the first time i felt i knew what i was doing

 even forgetting, at moments, about her
as i marveled at my own ability

 the next morning, we woke up
and it was a really fine moment for me
i had showed early promise
 and i figured i'd only get better

she rolled near me
and began to get things going again
 slowly building things up

it wasn't over instantly
 but it was close

 she laughed a little and said *ooh you were excited*

 but i knew what she meant

www.ingramcontent.com/pod-product-compliance
Lightning Source LLC
Chambersburg PA
CBHW051413290426
44108CB00015B/2268